Life Without Parole:

The Journey To
FREEDOM

A Step-by-Step Guide to Achieving Spiritual Freedom

JERRICA RUSSAW

Copyright © 2016 by Jerrica Russaw

All rights reserved. This book or any portion thereof may not be reproduced or used in any manner whatsoever without the express written permission of the publisher except for the use of brief quotations in a book review.

Limits of Liability and Disclaimer of Warranty

The author and publisher shall not be liable for your misuse of this material. This book is strictly for informational and educational purposes. The purpose of this book is to educate and entertain. The author and/or publisher do not guarantee that anyone following these techniques, suggestions, tips, ideas, or strategies will become successful. The author and/or publisher shall have neither liability nor responsibility to anyone with respect to any loss or damage caused, or alleged to be caused, directly or indirectly by the information contained in this book.

Views expressed in this publication do not necessarily reflect the views of the publisher.

Printed in the United States of America

ISBN: **978-0692756577**

Keen Vision Publishing, LLC

DEDICATION

Dear Ma,

I dedicate this book to you. You have taught me so much about life. Words cannot express how much I love and cherish you. I thank God for allowing me to have a mother who is a great example of how a Woman of God should be and doing exactly as you were instructed in Proverbs 22:6. I admire how nurturing, kind, humble, determined, and giving you are and I pray that one day I am half the mother you are for my children. Although you're my mother, our relationship has matured into something greater; you are truly my sister in Christ. We have prayed together, cried together, and even worshiped together. You have motivated me and encouraged me to trust God and to follow His commands. For that, I am grateful.

As I sit here writing this dedication, I can feel your

prayers all over me. I know it is because of your intercession that I am even able to be where I am today. You are so beautiful inside and out. I truly admire how graceful you are, even through the hard times. We have been through quite a bit together these past few years, but God has truly sustained us and blessed us even when we didn't deserve it.

I want to encourage you to continue to be the woman that God called you to be and no one else. God isn't through with you yet, and the best is yet to come for you. Surrender it all to God and watch him work it out.

Love you always,

Your Mema

ABOUT THE AUTHOR

Jerrica Russaw is first a servant chasing after Christ and his righteousness. She is originally from a small military town called Hinesville, Georgia. In late 2010, she moved to Tuskegee Institute, Alabama to pursue a higher education. In August of 2014, she graduated from the illustrious Tuskegee University with a Bachelor's of Science degree in Psychology. Jerrica has always enjoyed singing. During her tenure at TU, she was a dedicated member of the Tuskegee University Golden Voices Concert Choir under the direction of Dr. Wayne Barr. She now resides in Auburn, Alabama where she is an Outpatient Child Case Manager at East Alabama Mental Health Center. She is the founder of The Righteous Movement, which urges people of all ages to be the woman or man God has called them to be. She currently serves as a member of the Praise Team at White Street Baptist

Church under the leadership of Pastor Jamal Oliver. Her passion is to simply inspire others and help them through her testimony.

Contents

INTRODUCTION	1
STEP ONE	3
I'VE DECIDED	3
STEP TWO	15
RECOGNIZE THE CHAINS	15
STEP THREE	25
TIME TO TRAIN	25
STEP FOUR	47
AM I READY FOR THIS?	47
STEP FIVE	55
PUT THAT FAITH IN ACTION	55
STEP SIX	65
I HEAR THE CHAINS FALLING	65
STEP SEVEN	77
VICTORY IS MINE	77
FROM MY HEART, TO YOURS	81
A Word From The Author	81
THANK YOU'S	83

Life Without Parole: The Journey to Freedom　　　Jerrica Russaw

INTRODUCTION

Are you fed up with faking the funk? Are you tired of feeling like a prisoner to your life? Are you tired of being burdened by life's circumstances? THIS BOOK IS FOR YOU! Yes, you, the one who's reading this introduction. This book is an invitation to freedom for every person that has ever felt enslaved by any given situation or person. Just like you, I was burdened with bondage. I was held prisoner by the remnants of unresolved issues that affected my relationships, emotions, day-to-day functioning, and essentially my life. Like many of you, I searched for freedom in many different areas until I found myself broken, defeated, frustrated, enslaved, and burnt out. I continued to feel this way until I became determined to let God break me free from the bondage that held me hostage for so long. Now, I share my story, struggles, and triumphs of how I transitioned from figuratively serving a Life

Sentence to living a life of freedom. In a society that urges us to repay others for the evil committed against us, I discovered another strategy that yields a greater and everlasting reward. Join me on my journey to freedom as I challenge you to allow God to prepare a table in the presence of your enemies. This book is simple, challenging, and fulfilling. *Life Without Parole: The Journey To Freedom* is a step-by-step guide that teaches you how to: **Identify the things that have enslaved you for so long, Give whatever has held you hostage to Christ, Prepare for what to expect while on this journey, and Receive freedom and keep it.**

Well, enough of the small chat. Let's dig in!

STEP ONE

I'VE DECIDED

You have invested in this book because something has been eating away at the very essence of who you are for a while now. You've noticed that you do not enjoy the things you once enjoyed because they now seem dull. I'm sure you see instability in many different areas of your life. You have grown easily irritated and even get into these funky moods for no particular reason. You have searched and searched, but you cannot find peace anywhere. You cannot find peace in family, friends, relationships, possessions, or even success. You feel lost, and you do not know why. You have tried to fight back on your own, but you have grown frustrated because it feels like you're fighting a losing battle.

I am here to reassure you that you are not alone. I've been there. I have experienced those same emotions and frustrations. I went from an exuberant and energetic young lady to a bitter, negative, and angry little girl. I pushed people away who genuinely cared about me. The funny thing is that the entire time I was a devout member of the praise team and sang all week about how God was a healer, deliverer, conqueror, victor, etc., but I had not yet allowed Him to come into my life and be those things in my situation. Instead, I went on about my life and tried to handle things on my own. I thought this was something I could handle alone. Man, was I wrong!

This cloud of negativity sat right above my every move and overtook my life. It came into my heart and made itself extremely comfortable. Although I thought I could handle it, I was powerless against it. My decrees and declarations did not seem to work. My countless hours of tears were in vain. My prayers were ineffective, or *so I thought*. My worship sessions listening to the likes of Shauna Wilson,

Casey J, Hillsong, and Miranda Willis seemed pointless. I could not break free from this thing; it was attached to everything.

That is, until one day, I was exhausted and burnt out from trying to handle whatever this was that seemingly manifested itself in every aspect of my life. I sat on the floor of my little apartment and cried until there were no more tears left. I looked around, and the walls looked as though they were caving in on me. Problems were coming full force in every aspect of my life; my family and friends, my relationship, my church family, my coworkers, school, and everybody else seemed to have lost their minds. It was way too much for me to handle.

That's when a light bulb appeared over my head like in the cartoons. I knew what I had to do. The things my mother instilled in me as a child surfaced. I knew who had the peace I so desperately needed. Those many, many, MANY days of singing songs of victory began to really minister to me. The sermons I neglected to receive began to prick my heart and convict me. I knew I had to make a decision.

Those countless hours of prayer were not in vain. God was giving me the answers to my prayers the entire time, but I was too blind to receive them. Just like me, God had to humble you before He could elevate you to greater. Proverbs 18:12 (New International Version) says, *"Before a downfall the heart is haughty, but humility comes before honor."* God is not turning a deaf ear to you, and He is not looking the other way while you endure. He is beckoning you to come back to Him. He is opening His arms and trying to get your attention, but you are too proud to receive Him. You are so content with handling it on your own that you cannot see how you're worsening the situation and giving it the opportunity to destroy you.

You know what you have to do, but you must make the decision to do it. You have to give your situation and yourself to God completely. The Lord does not tolerate a lukewarm Christian. If you think I'm making this up, let's take it to the Word of God. Revelation 3:15-16 says, *"I know your deeds, that you are neither cold nor hot. I wish you were either one or the other! So, because you are lukewarm—neither hot nor cold—I am about to spit you out of my mouth."* What exactly is a lukewarm Christian? I'm so glad you asked. A lukewarm Christian is *"sometimey"*— a southern term describing a person that only comes around when they want something. Do you only pray when you are sad or when you need something? Do you only read your Bible when you are planning to ask for something? Do you only go to church on Easter or Christmas? BE HONEST with yourself.

If your answer to one or more of those questions is yes, then you may be considered lukewarm. Sorry, not sorry. When we are lukewarm in our relationship with God, we don't realize that we treat God like a genie in a bottle, instead of the King of kings and Lord of lords. We rub Him or attempt to fancy Him when it is beneficial to us. God is a gracious God, and the Bible says that His grace is sufficient **(2 Corinthians 12:9)**. We know that God still shows mercy to us in the midst of our filthy sinfulness, but are we using His grace as a crutch to continue to live any way we please?

Another approach to understanding how God loves us is to look at how God wants us to treat others. The Bible says to do unto others as you would have them do unto you **(Matthew 7:12)**. Does that not apply to how we treat God? Let's get real here. We all have that one friend that only comes around when they want or need something, how do we treat them? Do we show them love and compassion or do we check them or read them their rights? What if God treated us the same way according to how we treat Him? Not so cool anymore, huh?

God wants to help and deliver you, but you must first turn from your selfish ways, take up your cross, and follow Him. **(Matthew 16:24)** You must seek Him. The reward of seeking God is endless. The Bible says, *"Seek the Kingdom of God above all else, and live righteously, and he will give you everything you need."* **(Matthew 6:33)** Freedom, peace, and joy are included in that everything. The Bible also says, *"The lions may grow weak and hungry, but those who* *seek the Lord lack no good thing."* **(Psalm 34:10)** Now, I am not going to paint the picture that a life dedicated to God is nothing but flower beds and endless sunshine. If I told you that, I would be lying. SERVING GOD IS HARDWORK! I cannot stress that enough, but the scripture has ensured us that it is worth it and that the reward is everlasting and eternal. I'm sure you are puzzled and growing curious about what I am talking about, so let me break it down.

All my life, since I'm a PK (preacher's kid), I have heard preachers, teachers, and scholars say that salvation is free. As I matured in my faith, I realized that was only true to a certain extent. God sent his only Son, Jesus, down to be slain and to pay the ultimate cost for our salvation. Jesus was beaten and bruised to pay this cost. The cost was not paid in full until he carried an old rugged cross up to a hill called Calvary. On Calvary, He hung, bled, and died. Because Jesus is the real MVP, He got up with all power in His hands. So yes, your salvation costs you nothing but cost Him life. To keep your salvation costs your life. It costs your desires, will, goals, dreams, etc. Now I know that seems negative, but let's look at the reward of salvation.

I am sure you are reading this book like "Hold up, chick. It does not seem like it will profit me to follow this Jesus guy." Well, keep on reading. Just like you, one of the disciples asked Jesus the same question. Paraphrasing here, he says "We have left everything to follow you, what is in it for us? Jesus explained to the disciples that everyone who has left their homes, brothers, sisters, father, mother, children, or fields because of His name will receive a hundred times as much and will inherit eternal life. **(Matthew 19:19-30)** That means that anyone who has let go of the things that made them comfortable and stepped into the unknown will receive everything they ever desired and more. As an extra bonus, they receive eternal life. Boom! I told you it would be worth it.

Although God's rules to living a life for him are pretty simple, they seem outlandish because the world's way of thinking has been embedded into us from birth. That is why Scripture says that we were all born sinners, even from the moment of conception. **(Psalm 51:5)** Sin is what we know, it is comfortable, and it is deemed socially acceptable.

Let's compare! God says that we should abstain from sexual intercourse until marriage. The world encourages us to have sex with whomever we please, whenever we please. That is why it is so difficult for us to hold out until marriage. The world is constantly pushing sex, and it is hard work (let's be honest) to stay in the will of God. Not a good enough example? The Bible tells us that we should love our neighbor as ourselves. The world says that we should treat others how they treat us. The world teaches that if someone wrongs us, we should in turn wrong them. That is why we live in a society where people have no regard for others and their feelings. Can you think of an example of how the world's morals and God's morals differ? I'm sure you can! Write it below.

_____
_____
_____

Now is the time to choose to be hot or cold. Do you want to live a life for God or do you want to continue to live a life that is unfulfilling and filled with frustrations? Do you want to seek God first and allow Him to come into your heart and get things in order? Do you want to keep things the way they are? Are you ready for a change? If your answer is yes, and I hope it is, I advise you to go to your prayer closet.

No, it doesn't mean that you have to be in a physical closet. A prayer closet is just a place where you are alone with God. For me, it is my car. For you, it may be your actual closet, your bathroom, or your bed. If you don't have one, just think of a place where you can be totally alone with God and go there.

One thing I like to do is invite God in by playing some soft worship music. Some awesome examples are Shana Wilson and Hillsong. I sit and reflect on God. I reflect on how awesome He is, and how awesome He's personally been to me. It allows me to truly reverence and honor Him. So grab your phone, pull up some soft music, and say this prayer with me:

Father in the name of Jesus,

I am coming to you with a heavy heart. I have tried and tried to handle whatever this is on my own. I now realize that I cannot overcome this by myself, I need you to help me. God, come into my life and take over. I am choosing to turn from my selfish ways, pick up my cross, and follow you. God, I want to live for you. I want to surrender everything to you. I recognize that my salvation was paid for a long time ago by a man named Jesus. I accept that he died on the cross for my sins and resurrected with all power in his hands. God, I believe that you can and will sustain me and help me to endure. God, establish my steps and make my paths straight. Today, I choose to live for you and only you. I choose to not be a lukewarm Christian but to be a servant chasing after righteousness. But God, I need your help. I pray that you take my hand through this process and guide me to you. I want to live a bold life for you. God, I recognize that submitting to you will help me to resist the devil and watch him flee. You are gracious, all mighty, and an amazing God and I submit my life, my desires, and my will to you. Take everything God, because I just want you. From this day forward, I choose you and choose righteousness. Amen!

STEP TWO

RECOGNIZE THE CHAINS

Now that you have surrendered whatever this thing is to God, it's time to begin the journey to freedom. In order for you to fully achieve the freedom you are seeking, you must recognize and acknowledge exactly what has you bound. If you are like me, you have an idea of what the chains consist of. Is it a person or situation? Is it something that happened years ago that you are still holding onto? Write those things down below.

_____

_____

_____

_____

_____

Whelp, let me burst your bubble my friend. Those things that you mentioned are not the problem. I know you are sitting there like wait, what? I'll say it again: **That person or situation that you wrote above isn't the reason you are bound.** It is something deeper and much more powerful.

When I began my journey to freedom, I thought that the daddy issues that I was dealing with were the cause of why my life was spiraling out of control. My issues with my father seemed to spill over into other aspects of my life. I became defensive and guarded, thinking that everyone was against me because I continually had to defend myself against him. Something deep inside of me was letting me know that this was not the root and that I needed to consult with God for him to reveal it to me. So I prayed and prayed about it until one day, I was sitting in the women's group at my church, and the Lord placed a much needed revelation in my lap.

The being that I needed to take my freedom back from was not an earthly person. It was the devil and all of his workers. If you think I am crazy, turn your

Bible to Ephesians 6:12. It says, *"For we are not fighting against flesh-and-blood enemies, but against evil rulers and authorities of the unseen world, against mighty powers in this dark world, and against evil spirits in the heavenly places."* Yep, it's true. What I was bound by had nothing to do with my father, but it had everything to do with the true enemy. I am pretty confident that you are reading this book, accepting what I am saying but still believing that person or situation has something to do with your bondage. Don't fret we will deal with that later. BABY STEPS.

Write Ephesians 6:12 below.

_____
_____
_____
_____
_____

Now write it again on a piece of paper and put it up somewhere, where you can easily see it. Read it as much as you can and truly write it on the tablet of your heart. You will need the reminder later on in the process.

The enemy is a powerful being, yet powerless against God. We don't tend to think that the enemy is attacking us, because when we think of attacks, we think of what is visible to our eyes. The enemy excels because of this. We cannot see him, touch him, feel him, or physically fight him. Because of how stealthy he is, we often neglect to recognize his presence. We have to realize that he is there, and he is very busy. He is a master manipulator and the author of confusion. The enemy has a mission, and that is to steal, kill, and destroy. If we are honest with ourselves, he has already stolen our freedom, killed our joy, and has destroyed our relationships with others.

He wants to make living a life for God miserable. He is the reason why living for God is hard work! Was that emphasized enough, I'm not quite sure? I'm just going to say it one more time to make sure you understand: **The enemy is the reason why living for God is hard work.** He does his best to lure us to sin and cause us to stray away from the will of God. When we look at the Bible and read about the events that happened in those times, we can clearly see that the enemy tries to detour us from God because he knows what will happen when we stay faithful. This is evident in the genealogy of Christ. The enemy tried to detour those people because he knew that through them Jesus was coming. He knew that Jesus was going to save the world by shedding his blood. I can imagine the devil was pretty perturbed about that and made a decision to do something about it. So he set out to misguide, each and every person in the lineage of Jesus, but he failed.

The enemy is a tempter. He wants to misguide you so that you don't attempt to combat his schemes. He wants to lead you so far away from the source of your issues, that you don't even know where or how to start dealing with them. Sounds familiar? The devil is intentional about the things he does. The devil's schemes are not general; they are personal. He knows the things you have hidden deep down within the depths of your soul. He knows what will make you tick, and he knows how to distract you. That's why he is so good at what he does.

The same applies to our lives. The devil knew that if he kept me believing that the issue was my father, I would be distracted from him. He knew that as long as he kept me bound, he wouldn't have to worry about me writing a book on freedom to help others combat the attacks of the enemy and truly take back their freedom. *insert praise break* He knows that there is something greater within you, and he also knows that if you stay disconnected from God, you will be powerless against him. In Romans 8:38 it says, *"And I am convinced that nothing can ever separate us from God's love. Neither death nor life, neither angels nor demons, neither our fears for today nor our worries about tomorrow—not even the powers of hell can separate us from God's love."* Contradicting, right? Wrong.

Although nothing can separate us from the love of God, we often allow the enemy to separate God from our love. Isaiah 59: 2 says, *"Surely the arm of the Lord is not too short to save nor his ear too dull to hear. But your iniquities have separated you from your God; your sins have hidden his face from you so that he will not hear you."*

The enemy seeks to plant a seed of perversion that grows into discontentment, which leads to disobedience and ends in a disconnection. The perversion is the person or situation. He has already told us that the real enemy is not flesh and blood, the discontentment is the resentment that you have. The disobedience is the forgiveness that dwells in our hearts. The Bible says that we must forgive as God has forgiven us **(Ephesians 4:32)**, and it ends up disconnecting our love from God. John 14:15 says, *"If you love me, keep my commandments."* So our resentment, anger, bitterness, and malice against our sister or brother, creates a disconnection of God from our love because of our sin.

When we disconnect God from our love, we also disconnect ourselves from victory. We disconnect ourselves from freedom, joy, peace, patience, and most importantly endurance. That's why we become so angry and burnt out. We don't allow God to sustain and protect us. We have completely shut Him out our lives. We have allowed the enemy to make us believe that our "situation" is bigger than our God. We have given him free reign to come in and wreck our lives because we were not alert and anticipating his attacks.

List some adjectives that describe how disconnecting your love from God personally affects your life. My personal examples are bitterness, anger, and unforgiveness.

_____
_____
_____
_____
_____
_____

Now that you have composed a list, let's go to the feet of Jesus and lay those things there. Go to your prayer closet and say this prayer with me.

Father in the name of Jesus,

I come to You bearing all of the things that have held me hostage for so long. I come to You with my (list the things you listed previously.) These things do not line up with how You want me to live. I know that this stuff is from the enemy and are schemes to detour me from Your will and purpose for my life. I realize that the fight is not with man, but with spirits. I acknowledge and accept that I need You to help me and guide me so that I will win this battle. So I give it up to You. My heart is hard because of these things, but I want You to come in and make me a new. Although the enemy is powerful, Your power is insurmountable. I know that because I am reconnecting to You and because I am on a journey to declare my love for You, I am connected to Victory. I am connected to freedom. Although I may not have my victory now, I reverence You because I know it is on the way. Please give me the wisdom and strength to endure. In Jesus name, AMEN

STEP THREE

TIME TO TRAIN

If you think the enemy is going to hand you the keys to your freedom voluntarily, you are wrong. Don't be fooled into thinking that just because you have revealed him, he is going to release you without a fight. It's actually quite the contrary. He is going to send his best stuff your way to urge you to give up and give into him. Do not let this scare you. The victory is already won. In Isaiah 54:17, God reassures us that no weapon formed against us will prosper because we are His. He didn't say no earthly weapon, but he said no weapon. That includes the spiritual weapons of mass destruction of the enemy. Colossians 2:13-15 says, *"When you were dead in your sins and in the uncircumcision of your flesh,*

God made you alive with Christ. He forgave us of all our sins, having canceled the charge of our legal indebtedness, which stood against us and condemned us; he has taken it away, nailing it to the cross. And having DISARMED the powers and authorities, he made a public spectacle of them, TRIUMPHING over them by the cross." Long story short, because you are submitted to Christ and are a child of the King the battle is already won on your behalf. Although we know and are confident that the battles already won, we are still required to fight. I know it is a bit confusing, so let me break it down biblically.

Pull out your Bible and read 1 Samuel 17, which is the story of David and Goliath. Then answer the questions below based on what you read. (Make sure it is a translation that you can easily understand. I personally use the New Living Translation)

1. How big was Goliath?

2. Based on the text, is it safe to say that Goliath was a skilled warrior?

3. David showed his confidence in God by saying what?

4. What did David use to defeat Goliath?

5. Do you think that there was divine intervention involved in how Goliath was defeated?

The story of David and Goliath is an empowering passage. This passage, along with many popular stories in the Bible, is often disregarded for the power that it possesses. When we think of this story, we think of the face value we received in Sunbeam

Sunday school or as a child, without studying the text. Let's dig deeper into this story and retrieve the meat of the text.

At the beginning of this passage, we see the Philistine army gathered together waging war against Israel. Because Israel was considered the underdog in this matchup, a Philistine giant named Goliath comes out and taunts the Israeli army. This guy was huge, and so the Israeli army was afraid for they knew that they were doomed against the mighty forces of the Philistines. One day, Jesse, David's father, sent David to battle to deliver news to his brothers. When he got there, he saw this Giant taunting his people and being a young teenager without fear, David questioned Goliath and his power against God's people. Now David was a devout shepherd who was known to fight off lions and bears for his flock. Even this type of training was no match for the great warrior Goliath. I am sure David's brothers were puzzled and grew concerned about their little brother's boldness. I can hear them now, "Yo, David, chill! You are no match for him. If you do this, you're on your own we can't help you." But David had something they didn't possess; he had great faith in God. In his brother's minds, David was committing suicide, God saw something different and saw something that he could use; David's faith and his willingness. God knew that because of his willingness to defend his sheep from lions and bears, he would be willing to defend God's sheep, Israel, against the lion, Goliath. Because of his faith, he knew that David was perfect for this battle for he knew that through God the battle was already won. In reading the text, we see that because of David's faith, God gave him the power to defeat Goliath.

Just like David, you will have to go into battle to take back the freedom that the enemy stole from you. But God needs you to have faith in him to defeat the enemy. Do you have great faith? If so, it's time to train for battle. Before David stood against Goliath, he needed those lions and bears. The same applies to you. Before you stand against the enemy, you'll need to train on a smaller scale.

God allows things of smaller value to happen in our lives to train us or prepare us for what's to come. For me, it was instability in my relationship because they seemed to mimic my relationship with my father. He allowed certain situations happen with my church family to test how prepared I was. I didn't see it then, but now I see how he was using that to condition me for a bigger battle that was coming. Let's just say I was mauled by those lions and bears. I was defeated because I was bare and I didn't have any armor to protect myself.

Ephesians 6: 10-11 says, *"Be strong in the Lord and in the power of his might. Put on the whole armor of God, so that you can stand against the devil's schemes."* In the text, David put on Saul's armor, but it was too heavy for him, so he took it off. Trust and believe that although to the naked eye David seemed unguarded, he had on some armor, but this armor was special. We will look at this special armor that Paul talks about and describe the benefits of having this amazing armor.

Read Ephesians 6 and write down the specific pieces of armor that Paul illustrates below.

_____
_____
_____
_____
_____
_____
_____
_____
_____
_____
_____
_____

In Isaiah 59, it talks about how God saw that there was no one to stand against the enemy. So he stood and put on some armor to prepare for battle. When the Apostle Paul writes about this armor, he is not just talking about any kind of armor, but he is illustrating the impregnable armor of the Almighty God.

When he begins to speak of this powerful armor, I found it odd that he first spoke about a belt. Of all of the pieces to bring us in with, he starts with a belt. In order for me to truly understand its significance, I had to understand and learn about the armor of a soldier, a Roman solider to be specific.

In that time, which was between 70-80 AD, a belt was identified as cingulum or balteus. It was crucial to how effective a soldier's armor was. The belt was significant, but what it held was even more powerful. The belt had a pocket or holder known as the scabbard connected to it. This scabbard was very important to battle because it held the sword. Another role of the balteus was that it also had leather straps hanging from it to protect the lower body. Last but certainly not least, the belt girded or secured all of the other pieces of the armor and helped hold them together. How does this relate to God?

The Belt of God is called the Belt of Truth for a distinct purpose. The Truth is God and everything thing that comes from him. In John 14:6, we see

Christ declaring that he is the truth. So if God is truth, then that means that the word that he sent is also the truth. That is verified through scripture in John chapter 17, verse 17which says, *"Sanctify them by the truth; your word is truth."*

It is important that you gird yourself with the word of God because it is the word of God that helps you withstand the attacks of the enemy. It is pertinent that you know that in Deuteronomy 28:13 it says that you are the head and not the tail, and if you follow His commands you will always be on top. You don't know if you don't gird yourself with truth. For this particular reason Deuteronomy 6: 8 says that you should tie them (the word of God) as symbols on your hands and bind them to your foreheads. Although Jews in that time took God literally and had boxes containing scripture tied to their arms or forehead, God meant it figuratively. He wants you to write the word on the tablet of your heart. For it is the truth that sets you free, John 8:32. So it's time to invest in a Bible, that you can clearly understand and a journal, where you can write down the things that the Spirit will reveal to you and scriptures that may pertain to your situation.

If you are not girded in truth, you are giving the enemy leeway to lead you astray. For instance, when Eve was approached by the enemy because she was not girded in the truth of what God said, she was lead to disobey God. It is important that you know the word for yourself because the enemy takes what is almost right and lures us to disobedience. He won't be able to succeed if you are girded in truth and know the Word of God for yourself.

The second piece of armor that Paul illustrates in Ephesians 6 is the Breastplate of Righteousness. The breastplate of a Roman soldier protected vital organs, such as the heart. The same applies to the Breastplate of Righteousness.

Without this critical piece of armor, one of the most vital spiritual organs will be left susceptible to damage; the heart. In Proverbs 4:23 it says to guard your heart for out of it flows the issues of life. To guard your heart, you must have on the Breastplate of Righteousness. So this thing that has you bound is a reflection of how the enemy has corrupted your heart. Don't fret; God is a restorer, and if you let Him in, he will serve the enemy an eviction notice. Let's look at righteousness and how we can put this piece of holy armor on.

Righteousness is simply the things that God commands of us. Psalm 119:172 says, "May my tongue sing your word, for all your commands are righteous." When we do the things that are required of us, we are bearing the breastplate of righteous. That includes doing the righteous thing in the face of adversity for this breastplate will help to protect you from the blows of the enemy. When worn the things that once pierced your heart become ineffective and powerless. That person or situation that you listed before as the culprit, the devil will no longer be able to use it or them to get to you because his attacks are no longer effective.

The third pieces of armor are the shoes of the preparation of the gospel peace. Shoes are important to anyone in any situation. Let's all go back to the day when we stumped our toe on the side of the couch because we didn't have anything to protect our feet. If you're dramatic like me, you see the light and hear the Lord calling your name because the pain is so bad your life is basically over. Now imagine a Roman soldier with a full body of armor on, but somehow he has forgotten his shoes. Odd right? Now imagine trying to fight someone in battle stepping in debris, rocks, etc. You probably won't get very far. The same way that the shoes protect your feet, the shoes of the preparation of the gospel of peace protect you. These shoes allow you to step freely without worry about damage to your feet. They also allow you to give your full attention to what's in front of you instead of what's below you. These shoes help you to be totally fixated on Jesus so that you are not distracted from the task at hand. This is where the enemy has succeeded. Instead of us fixating our eyes on Christ, we are so worried about who wronged us and how it made us feel. The enemy strategically takes our attention from God, because when we are not focused on Christ, we won't be able to follow his direction to victory.

The Roman soldiers often wore shoes that had nails on the bottom, for the purpose of keeping the soldier planted in the ground below when otherwise it would be easy to lose his balance. God wants us to plant ourselves in the Gospel or good news, so that when the battle commenced we can stand firm. In Matthew 7: 24-27 it speaks on the wise and unwise builders. It says that wise man takes the Word of God and lays down a firm foundation, so that when the winds blow his house doesn't fall. We are the house, and we must root ourselves in the firm foundation of the Word of God to have peace in the face of adversity.

The fourth piece of armor is the Shield of Faith. This particular item is different from the rest because you put on the belt, the breastplate, and the shoes, and they hold themselves up essentially, but the Shield of Faith is something that you must hold up and raise. After watching movies like 300, it is easy to picture this shield as a circular metal contraption. The Roman soldiers had something that was different. This shield, in that day known as a Scutum, was rectangular. Because of this shape, the soldier was greatly protected by his shield. It also contained a knob known as a Boss, which allowed the soldiers to not only protect himself from various blows from the enemy, but it also allowed the soldier to knock their opponent back a couple of steps.

In this same aspect, Faith is detrimental to retrieving our victory. The biblical definition of faith is the evidence of things hoped for and the evidence of things not seen. You may not see how God is going to move on your behalf and hand you your freedom back, but Faith says I don't care about what I can't see because I know that he is going to work it out. Faith is stepping out on faith and writing a book on the tools needed to retrieve the freedom that the Devil has stolen from you, not knowing the first thing about book writing. Faith believes that God is using this young country girl from the sticks of Georgia known as "Buzzard Root," to help you through what may seem like the hardest season of your life.

A physical shield protects the body from deadly blows; faith protects our spiritual life when everything seems to be failing. Faith tells your situation about your God. Matthew 17:20 says, "Because you have so little faith. Truly I tell you, if you have faith as small as a mustard seed, you can say to this mountain, Move from here to there, and it will move. Nothing will be impossible for you." Faith is Daniel in the Lion's Den (Daniel 6), faith is the Three Hebrew Boys (Daniel 3), faith is the Woman with the issue of blood (Luke 8), and faith is David and Goliath (1 Samuel 17). Faith is saying I'm free in the midst of your bondage, believing that the Devil will unbind you at your command because you are connected to the power of God.

The fifth piece of armor is the Helmet of salvation. The use of a Helmet is universal; it protects the head. Salvation means to be delivered from sin and its consequences. To receive salvation Peter says, "Repent, and let everyone of you be baptized in the name of Jesus Christ for the remission of sins; and you shall receive the gift of the Holy Spirit." Our salvation is considered a gift because God sent down his only son to pay the price for our salvation.

Jesus was persecuted and beaten for us. But it doesn't stop there; Jesus bore the burden of carrying a cross up to a hill call Golgotha, which means the place of the skull. He was so committed to ensuring salvation for us that he refuse to drink wine mixed with gall, which in those days served as an anesthetic. He wanted to feel the pain and pay the entire cost. Although he was powerful enough to save himself and smite everyone else, he knew that we needed a savior. So he allowed them to nail him to that cross and raise him. After hours of torment from being suspended on the cross, he voluntarily gave up his life. Three days later, just like he declared, he was resurrected and because of his sacrifice we have salvation. (Matthew 27:32 – Matthew 28) This is just a snippet of the truth about what our salvation costs.

This salvation is used as a helmet in the armor of God because it protects our minds from discontentment, discouragement, and despair in this world. In Romans 12:2 the Bible says, "Do not conform to the pattern of this world, but be transformed by the renewing of your mind." As Christians, we were chosen to live a life that is different from the world. Yes, we live in the world, but we must allow the truth to change not only our way of thinking but also the way we live should not be like the world. We are called to cultivate and eventually develop a mind that resembles Christ. (Philippians 2:5) This is why it is so crucial to have the word of God written on the tablets of our hearts and bound on our foreheads.

The enemy is not a fan of us actually operating in salvation, so he does everything in his power to destroy our faith. 1 Peter 5:8 says, "be alert and of sober mind. Your enemy the devil prowls around like a roaring lion looking for someone to devour." The devil is constantly searching for a new way to devour your faith, but if you wear the helmet of Salvation, it will protect your thoughts from the temptations and deceptions of the enemy to disobey God.

How do I wear this helmet? Well, it's simple; you must believe and keep your eyes fixated on Jesus. The salvation that you want is simply to enter God's kingdom. When this is constantly on your mind, then it makes suffering right now worth it. So when you are constantly thinking about your heavenly home, no matter how malicious or vicious that the attacks of the enemy are, we are confident in the notion that if we remain faithful to God, we will inherit a heavenly home.

As I wrote this book, I often pictured the armor in its carnal sense. I imagined this great armor that glistened with royal jewels and its gold was as bright as the son. (Pun intended) I imagined a great soldier preparing for battle putting on each piece and making sure it was secure. I imagined him stepping to his opponent, but wait he was missing something. He had this great armor, but what was he going to offensively fight with? That is when I pictured the sixth piece of the holy armor of God, the Sword of the Spirit.

Although the Roman soldier had other weapons such as daggers, spears, and darts, the sword was its main defensive tool. Paul strategically only mentioned the sword as being a part of the armor of

God. The sword of the spirit is simply the Word of God.

God's word is so powerful because as exclaimed in Psalm 119:105, his word is a lamp unto our feet and a light unto our path. God's Word is a light that shines on everything we do, exposing what's good from what's bad. Because of this in Hebrews 4:12 says, "For the word of God is alive and active. Sharper than any double-edged sword, it penetrates even to dividing soul and spirit, joints and marrow; it judges the thoughts and attitudes of the heart." With the word you cannot only challenge the enemy, but you can also expose his plans to attack you and deflect his blows to your faith. Christ himself even did this in Matthew chapter 4, when the enemy tried to tempt him. The same way that Christ used the word of God to deflect the attack of the enemy, we must do the same when we are on the journey to retrieving our victory.

Paul concludes speaking on this comprehensive and intricate armor of God, by highlighting prayer. He says, "And pray in the Spirit on all occasions with all kinds of prayers and requests." (Ephesians 6:18) Prayer is the thing that keeps each piece of armor individually and collectively strong. Prayer is when you get intimate with God and ask for his spirit to guide you to fight the good fight. The Bible says to ask, and you shall receive. So therefore if we don't ask for wisdom in defeating the enemy how will we receive it? Let me kick it up a step, how do you expect to receive this armor if you do not consult the person who it belongs to?

A strong prayer life is very important in this Christian journey. Your prayer life is a direct correlation with your relationship with Christ. If we think about forming relations, if we don't communicate and get to know the person then how can we have a relationship with them? The same applies to God. We do not want to fall into the trap of being Genie in the Bottle saints.

If you are like many people, you feel as though you do not know how to pray. Prayer is simply a conversation with God. When I took on the undertaking on learning how to pray, I looked at an often looked over prayer in the Bible, which is the prayer of Christ himself in John 17. Most of us begin our prayers or conversations by immediately asking something of God, without even saying hello. In this chapter, Christ began his prayer by reverencing God. Then he began to ask God for the desires of his heart. God wants to talk to you and not just take requests from you.

War Room, a movie about the benefits of having an active prayer life, helped me to work on my prayer life. It also helped me to realize the power of posting different tidbits of the truth where I can easily see it. Seeing the scriptures often allows those scriptures and revelations to get down on the tablet of our hearts and also helps us to remind our self of God's promises.

So right now, I want you to write down each piece of the armor of God, along with a scripture that correlates to it and post it somewhere you can easily see it. Read it and meditate on it often. Write on the tablet of your hearts.

Now construct a prayer specific to what you are going through. Research some scriptures to include in this prayer to help back up what you are saying. Write it below.

STEP FOUR

AM I READY FOR THIS?

The enemy knows that you are preparing to take back everything he stole from you, and he is conjuring up a plan to break you. He knows your weak spots and the most sensitive areas of your life. Because he is so calculated, he will attack those areas when you are most vulnerable. He will attack those areas when he knows when he can get the most impact.

I know this because he did it to me. To be totally transparent, the enemy knew that my relationship with my father was a sensitive spot for me. My father and I were as thick as thieves growing up. If you saw him, I was shortly behind trying to be just like him. He was the cool dad. Although his job caused him to travel, he always made sure that the times that we shared were of value.

The enemy knew I valued that relationship and he also knew that through the tearing down of that close bond he could use it to destroy me. Whelp over the course of about 5 – 6 years, my father and I's relationship dwindled down to a pretty unhealthy one. It hurt me to my core and left me angry. Outwardly I lashed out and pushed everyone who tried to get close to me away, while inwardly I was crying for help.

I was not rooted in the word of God, nor did I have a strong prayer life. The only thing I had was a void and a quick tongue. I did not know what the Bible said about me, better yet the enemy. I did not know that this was a plot to keep me from the will God. All I saw and all I knew was that the man that I had a lot of faith in betrayed me and my trust.

I tried to move past it, but it seemed like when everything was copasetic; BOOM, here we go again. I was on an emotional roller-coaster. It was an involuntary ride that I couldn't escape from. It consumed my life like a burning fire. Until one day, God did something that would change my life. He held up a mirror to my faith and told me to take a self-analysis of my life and my faith.

Just like me, God is telling you to self-inventory of your faith. You want victory but do you have the faith to receive it? Do you have the faith that it takes to fight to get it? Do you? If you are completely honest with yourself, the answer to these questions are either no or maybe. For me, at the time it was a definite, no. We've already established that the Bible says, "Faith is the substance of things hoped for and the evidence of things not seen." (Hebrews 11:1) But can we honestly say that although our freedom isn't tangible at this very moment, we have enough faith to continue to hold onto the promises of God?

Throughout the Bible, we can find stories attesting the necessity of faith in any situation. There is one story that sticks out personally, and that is easily relatable to how bound we feel. That story is entitled, "The Woman with the issue of blood." If you have your Bibles, and I hope you do, (that's that Southern Baptist spilling out), I'm going to ask you to read Luke 8:42-48.

This story is reminiscent of my own struggle with freedom and should be similar to yours as well. This woman was bound by an issue of blood for twelve years. She traveled from doctor to doctor and tried every method of healing, but no one could heal her. Because of her great faith in God, she knew that if she could just touch the edge of Jesus' cloak, she would receive the healing that she so desired. She managed to get close enough to do so and something amazing happened, she was instantly healed. Jesus felt some of his power being released, so he asks who it was that touched him. Now he was in a crowd, so it's safe to say that he was constantly being touched. Jesus knew that this touch was different. The woman came forward and admitted that she was the culprit, but to her surprise, the Lord commended her great faith.

Just like the woman with an issue of blood, we have dealt with the burden of bondage for quite a while.

We have gone from person to person to be healed, but in the words of Mr. Kanye West, "You don't have the answers Sway!" God needed us, just like he did the woman in this story, to get to the point where we realized that if we're just able to sit at his feet and in His presence, we will be healed. One thing that we have to really look at is the simple fact that this woman wasn't healed because she touched Jesus' clothes, because if that were the case, then the entire crowd would've been healed. She was healed because of her faith.

This battle that you are planning and training to embark on, the outcome is contingent upon your faith. If you have weak faith, then you will be weak in the presence of your enemy. If you have weak faith, then you won't allow that armor that we spoke of earlier to work on your behalf. If you have weak faith, then you block God's power from entering your situation.

Let me burst that bubble one more time. If you are honest with yourself, you have weak faith because if you didn't, you wouldn't be reading this book on freedom. You may feel like you are the only one but sweetheart let me tell you, you're not. If you were then, the Bible wouldn't say, "If we only had faith as small as the size of a mustard seed…" I don't know if you've seen a mustard seed lately, but those things are ridiculously small. Plus, I don't see CNN reporting on mountains throwing themselves into the sea, so that tells me that we all have areas in our faith that we need to work on.

How do I strengthen my faith? Wow, are you in my head or something because your questions are on point! To strengthen your faith, you must be intentional about it. If you wanted to strengthen your legs, your abs, or your arms, you have to consistently work at it. That means working out and eating appropriately right? Well, my friend, the same applies to your faith. To strengthen your faith, you have to consistently work at it. You have to wake up every day praying for faith and acting in faith, which is your workout, while feeding your spiritual man, which means reading your word.

It's time to mature those spiritual muscles. Now is not the time to be modest, it's time to get down to the nitty-gritty of our hearts and allow God to throw out the residue left by the enemy. I'm sure that there are areas in your life where you can easily identify that you need to strengthen your faith. Write them below and research scriptures that pertain to those areas and write those down beside it.

_____
_____
_____
_____
_____
_____

If you haven't realized by now, there is a method to my madness. I asked you to research scriptures because you are going to use them to speak life into problem areas. Using the areas that you have listed and the scriptures that you have researched, craft a prayer to God, asking him to help you to strengthen these areas of your faith. Also, giving him free reign to come in and take over. Write your prayer below.

STEP FIVE
PUT THAT FAITH IN ACTION

ATTACK!!!! It's go time. The enemy has had possession of your freedom for way too long. Now is not the time to crumble under pressure, but it's time for you to put that faith into action. In Step 2, I asked you to document scriptures that pertained to your bondage. This is where you'll need it. The enemy is waiting for you and is in possession of spiritual weapons of mass destruction. His number one goal is to intimidate you and cause you to not only doubt God, but also doubt what God has birthed in you. What he has obviously forgotten is that he was defeated, is defeated, and will always be defeated.

This battle will not be easy. It will probably be one of the hardest things that you will have to endure, simply because it requires a lot of discipline. The enemy will use those areas where you're most vulnerable and wreak havoc on them. He wants you to physically fight the situation and not use your spiritual weapons because you can't harm him physically.

When I went through my battle, I found out some pretty devastating news about who my father was. It crushed me and fueled my anger even more. At this point, I was exhausted from trying to fight this situation physically I decided to try something new. Instead of checking him on it, I made an intentional decision to fight with my spiritual weapons and that was prayer and scripture. This is where those scriptures that you've written down come in handy; they are like bullets in a gun. They can be used to stop the enemy dead in his tracks and making him second guess who he's messing with.

During this time, there were plenty of times when I could've laid into my father's character, but I decided to pray for him instead of judging him. Romans 3:23 says, *"For all have sinned and fall short of the glory of God."* I had to ask myself a question, did that verse not pertain to my father as well? One of the Ten Commandments is to treat others as you would want to be treated. Another question popped up. If I were in his shoes would I want to be forgiven or would I want my past continuously thrown in my face? It will be difficult, but you have to start seeing things through spiritual eyes and not through the lenses of anger and hurt. That is easier said than done, trust me I know. That is why it is so important to have an active and healthy prayer life. We have already established that if you believe you will receive, so if you believe God to soften your heart towards that person or situation, he will do it. So your charge is simply to stay positive and optimistic. Don't dwell on the negative, because if you do, it will eventually dwell in you.

In the previous chapter, we discussed how the enemy will use any way he can to get to you. That any way includes your children, family, friends, school, church, etc. Don't be surprised when situations arise from the abyss. When I decided to write this book, my mother became very ill and a thought leading me to prepare for her death crossed my mind. I was totally distraught and unfocused, until one day I just snapped out of the stronghold the enemy had over me. I spoke to her sickness and consulted the best doctor there is, and that is Jesus Christ. You cannot become distracted by your surroundings but instead, put that faith into action. I knew that God could heal my mother, but I lacked action behind my faith. When I put action behind my faith, I began to pray against the enemy. In doing so, slowly but surely my mother's condition got better.

James 2:17 says, *"Faith by itself, if it is not accompanied by action, is dead."* Faith and action are synonymous; you cannot have one without the other. I previously used a scripture that talked about what faith the size of a mustard seed could do to a mountain. I have a question, how will you know that you have faith as big or small as a mustard seed if you never act and tell the mountain to move? I have another question. How would David have beaten Goliath, if he never stepped out on his faith? These things would be impossible. That is why faith and action are stressed in this particular portion of the Bible. `

On many accounts where the people asked God for healing, God tested their faith. One particular account derives from Matthew chapter 15 verses 21-28. This particular portion of the New Testament speaks of the faith of a Canaanite Woman. Jesus was known for performing miracles. Everywhere he went, crowds gathered around him. One day, a woman approached him and begged him to deliver her demon-possessed daughter. The text says that Jesus said nothing in response to this woman and his squad, the disciples, came to him and told him that he needed to send her on her way. Strategically, because let's be honest Jesus knew exactly what was going on, he says to this woman that he was sent to the lost sheep of Israel. During this time the Israelites and the Gentiles were not allowed to intermingle. Jesus knew that but he wasn't being uppity, as we would modernly call it, he was testing this woman. Continuing with the story, she responds to his seemingly rude comment by kneeling and saying

Lord help me. He replies in riddle form and says, "*It is not right to take the children's bread and toss it to the dogs.*" Israelites were considered God's people so they would have figuratively been at the table feasting on the mercy of Jesus because they were his people, while the Gentiles were considered as lowly as dogs. She replies to him by saying yes but even the dogs eat the crumbs that fall from their master's table, meaning that even if she has to get leftover mercy, it would surely be more than enough to heal her daughter. This woman had great faith because although she knew that she wasn't deemed one of God's chosen people, she recognized and believed that even the figurative crumbs would have been enough. God tested her faith, and he'll do the same to us.

Another major example of God testing someone's faith is the story of Job. Job was a very wealthy man who had land, livestock, servants, and a beautiful family; until it all changed. God allowed Satan to attack Job to test his faith. Now God didn't allow him to kill Job, but some pretty devastating things did happen. Through these trials and hardships the devil put him through, Job lost everything. He lost his health, his servants, his children, his livestock, and his wealth. The enemy even used his wife to try to convince him to commit suicide. And if that wasn't bad enough, his friends came and gave him some pretty bad advice. But because of Job's faithfulness, God restores him. In other words, Job stayed faithful during hard times and God rewarded him for that. I am sure there were plenty of times when he wanted to give up or let go, but he had to remind himself of the promises of God. We have to get to that point in our relationship with Christ, where no matter what comes our way we are faithful to God. The enemy tempts us and uses those around us to persuade us to commit spiritual suicide. Spiritual Suicide is simply turning our backs on Christ and accepting the wages for our sins. In Romans 6:23 it says, *"The wages of sin is death and gift of God is eternal life."* I don't know about you, but I don't want to endure the wages of my sins.

Another important aspect of this fight is the troops that you have around you. You need to evaluate the people that you have fighting beside and with you. You're going to need someone to hold you accountable and someone who can lead you towards Christ and not away from him. During my battle, I was surrounded by some not so great friends. It made it very hard to fight effectively because I had people in my ear persuading me to handle it from the world's perspective, instead of them directing me towards Christ. It wasn't until I purged my circle that I was able to fight effectively. It is very pertinent that you pray and ask God to send you friends that will uplift you, pray for you, encourage you, and motivate you. It makes all the difference when you have friends that are capable of fighting for you when you may not be able to fight for yourself. So evaluate those friends of yours and make sure that they are capable of fighting for you, instead of creating opposition and fighting against you. Now I'm not saying that you have to kick them completely out of your life. I'm just simply advising you to distance yourself from them during this portion of the journey.

The only way to win is to fight with scripture and prayer. When things get tough pray and ask God for strength, then go to the word find a scripture that speaks of strength. When things are great pray just as hard as you would if they weren't. During my personal journey, I made the mistake of falling off when things were good. BIG MISTAKE! That's when the enemy sneaks you and takes you by surprise. Someone once told me a long time ago "Nothing hurts worse than something you weren't expecting." To be honest, that's very true.

A personal example is that after some time of fighting for freedom, my relationship with my father made drastic improvements. It seemed like we were well on our way to having the relationship that we had when I was younger. Whelp, one day we got into a huge argument, and there I was hurt again. I didn't expect it, and it most definitely threw me for a couple of loops. Once again, I was thrown off course. If I was prayed up and continuously clinging to

Christ, I would have known that it was just the enemy trying to get me off my path towards freedom. Prayerfully and through the encouragement of friends, I picked myself up, got it together, and started the journey once more. It took a couple of times, LOL.

This portion requires you to be steadfast, unmovable, and always abounding in the word of the Lord. It helps you to encourage yourself in those times of doubt and frustration. So keep your eyes on Christ and He will lead and sustain you through this process.

STEP SIX

I Hear The Chains Falling

During this portion, life is finally looking up. The things that once plagued your life are no longer effective. The things that seemed like a nuisance around your neck, no longer bother you. You're winning, and everything seems to be going great. So obviously you've won, right, because the enemy isn't pestering you anymore? WRONG. This is the time where the enemy executes his grand finale.

During my time, I was doing well. My life was prospering, and my situation was improving. That's when the enemy let out his best scheme ever. He attacked like never before. He attacked everything at once. It was so much at one time. There I was broken once more; I told you it took a couple of tries.

I was broken down and became frustrated like never before. If I can just be brutally honest, it seemed like I was worse than when I began the journey. So how did this happen? It was simply because I was fooled by the mirage of freedom and slacked on the things that allowed me to get this far on my journey.

I didn't pray like I used to and I definitely stopped putting on the armor of God. My life was so busy. I didn't purposely slack off; I just had so much going on. That's where we mess up. We get too busy to make time for God. We lose sight of the battle, because of our false sense of freedom. This faulty freedom leaves us vulnerable. It leaves us open to fall into the trap of the enemy because we think we have already defeated him. In all actuality, we haven't. This is how the enemy gets us; he waits until we no longer watch for him. Luke 4: 1-13 confirms that after the enemy had failed at getting Jesus to tempt God, he left and waited for the opportune time. Although victory is in sight, be watchful. The Bible says that enemy is constantly prowling looking for those that he can devour. (1 Peter 5:8) An old preacher said, "If you stay ready, then you won't have to get ready." Sweetheart, stay ready and armored with the armor of God. Pray harder, read more, and seek him continuously. This portion doesn't require a lot of instruction because, at this point, you have the tools. You just have to be planted in God and not potted for a moment.

At this point of the journey, I want you to put this book down, pray, and ask the Holy Spirit to come in and takeover. Don't skip this step or just read past it; it's pertinent that you do this!!!!!!!This step is going to require you to fight the hardest.

I want you to think of the situation or person that you thought of at the beginning of this book. Construct a letter to that person and ask them to forgive YOU. Yep, you read it right. Ask THEM to FORGIVE YOU. When the Lord instructed me to do this, I was like but God he should be apologizing to me not the other way around. Well the Lord got me all the way together and made me get my life. He said I want you to read a couple of things. So if you have your Bible's and I sure hope you do. Turn to

Ephesians 4:29-32. Ephesians is in the New Testament immediately following Galatians and proceeding Philippians. Read it and write it in your own words below.

_____
_____
_____
_____
_____
_____

Let's take this one verse at a time. Verse 29 says that we should not speak negatively, but in everything, we must speak life and not death. If you are like I was about my father, every time someone would bring him up, I would go on this tangent as to how horrible he was. I was so angry and bitter that it began to spill over into my relationships with others, whether romantic or otherwise. I wasn't trusting, and I had a huge guard up towards everyone. In my mind, I needed to be this way so that no one would hurt me like that again. Well to my surprise, not really, I wasn't that great at it. I ended up being too emotionally vulnerable with everyone that inquired, and I unloaded all my issues on them, which in turn drove them away. No one wants to be around some who is constantly carrying a cloud of negativity around with them. I know I don't! Well God checked me on that and caused me to really take my issues to him because let's be 100, no one else can resolve and restore like he can.

Verse 30 says we shouldn't grieve the Holy Spirit. That verse may be a bit confusing for you, so I am going to break it down to you. The Holy Spirit is grieved when we don't follow God, and we neglect or negate his word(s) to us. He has just told us to keep our negative thoughts to ourselves, so if we turn around and continue that negative talk, then we are grieving the Spirit. If you read what was said early in the last chapter, "the wages of sin is death, but the gift of God is eternal life." So if we look at this, the spirit is grieving because we are choosing death over life. HA!!!!!!!! I'll say it again: The spirit is grieving because we are choosing death over life.

What do you choose? And if you feel as though you just need to speak to someone about it and get something off your chest, I strongly suggest that you get on your knees and go to the one that can actually help you.

Verse 31 says to get rid of that bitterness, anger, slander, malice, etc. When we rid ourselves of those things, it becomes a lot easier to keep our deadly tongues off that person. Accept it or not, that person is God's child just as you are. BOOM. Just as God is patient with us when we choose to wrong him and abandon him, he expects us to be the same for his children.

Verse 32 just brings it all together; it says that we must continue being compassionate, kind, and most importantly FORGIVING. We have to forgive that person, even when they don't want to be forgiven. Jesus was beaten, battered, spat at, and insulted for the very people that he died for and still died gracefully and full of compassion. We crucify Christ each day that we neglect and disobey him for our own selfish desires, and he is interceding on our behalf saying, "Father, forgive them for they don't know what they are doing."

At this point, I was super convicted, but he said, "Nope, you're not humbled enough." So let's head on over to Colossians 3:12-14. You don't have that far to go from Ephesians. Colossians is right after Philippians and before 1 Thessalonians. You know the drill, read and write below.

_____
_____
_____
_____
_____
_____

Verse 12 talks about how the chosen people of God (you) should be compassionate, kind, humble, gentle and patient. Sounds familiar huh? Of all of those things listed patient stuck out to me the most. When dealing with someone that has hurt us, we often negate the call for patience. We want our apology, our breakthrough, everything upon our command; instead of having patience as God has commanded of us. Dear Friend listen to me. Just because you have compassion for others, doesn't mean they will have compassion for you. Just because you are kind to others, doesn't necessarily mean that they will, in turn, be kind to you. The latter portion of Matthew 5:39 confirms this when it says, "If anyone slaps you on the right cheek, turn to them the other cheek also." Meaning if anyone wrongs you, don't retaliate. The purest example of someone in the Bible doing this is Jesus Christ himself. While in custody, Jesus was beaten, spat upon, and insulted but he never said anything. He remained graceful and compassionate. While He hung on the cross as people that once praised him insulted him he says, "Father, forgive them, for they do not know what they are doing." (Matthew 23:34) If the only sinless human on this planet had to turn the other cheek when he could have easily called down the angels to fight on his behalf, what makes us so dignified and so much better that we don't think that we would have to do the same thing as well? Are we so much better than Christ that we feel like we shouldn't have to go through similarities in the struggle? Well Hunny chile, let me burst that bubble we aren't.

Verse 13 says that we must bear with each other and forgive as God has forgiven us. The first thing that this verse tells us to do is to bear with one another, meaning to endure. Well, my friend, this road is not going to be easy, and everybody is not going to be in line with the word of God, but as Christians is it our duty to bear with one another. Meaning that we must be patient with them, even when they are acting cray-cray. We have to continue to show the love of Christ, through their mess and ours to. The next thing it instructs us to do is to forgive as God has forgiven us. The Greek word for forgive is charizomai, which derived from the word charis that means grace. We must be gracious with our forgiveness. I acknowledge and fully understand that it is hard to truly forgive someone, who doesn't want to be forgiven. I get it, and I totally understand, but God calls us to forgive as he has forgiven us. We aren't the best either, and we have hurt God time and time again, yet he still forgives us as if it was our first time doing whatever we did.

The last step to truly forgiving someone is to tell them that you do so! AHHHHH what? Yes, ma'am/sir, if you thought that this was going to end easily then you're mistaken. This portion of the process is when you have to use the tools presented early on and exercise your faith. The sooner, the better. The longer you wait, the more time you're giving the enemy to consume your thoughts and talk you out of it.

First things first, seek God and request the presence of his spirit to guide you in what to say and also what not to say. (Take a minute and seek God's face.)

Then, we must construct a game plan. God is a prepared God who seeks prepared people. So let's take a moment and construct a concise apology. When I say concise, I mean summarized and not necessarily short. It's time to get real with the person and show the Love of Christ. So break out some paper and a pen. Construct a letter to whomever it is that you thought plagued your life and sincerely apologize. Apologize for the things that you have done and recognize what you could have done to improve the situation, not worrying about what they should've done. The most important part is to think with your spiritual mind, instead of your fleshly mind. YOU CAN DO THIS!!!! If you need a little more help and a push, read Luke 6:27-42.

STEP SEVEN

VICTORY IS MINE

How do I know I'm free? Well, my friend 2 Corinthians 3:17 indicates that wherever the Spirit of the Lord is, freedom is there also. Correct me if I'm wrong but in the last chapter, I asked you to pray for who to dwell with you? The spirit right? Uh Huh. John 8:36 says, "So if the Son sets you free, you will be free indeed." This entire book, I have been stressing the need for you to be connected to the son and how pertinent it is for you to be in his word, continuously having a dialogue with him, and avidly pursuing his presence. With that being said, I don't know about you, but it's time to have a sho 'nuff good praise party. AHHHHHHHH!!!!!! Break out the bubbly, Sparkling

Cider of course. God did it. He gave you the freedom that you so desperately desired. With him as your commander, Chief of Staff, as everything he has lead you to victory. You have successfully graduated from a lukewarm Christian to a Fiery Solider of the Kingdom. God has granted you the true desire of your heart, and that was to be free. HOW DOES IT FEEL? Great, huh? Whelp, don't get too comfortable, sweetheart, the work never stops. We must celebrate only for a moment keeping in mind that God wants us to go higher in him.

Although this was a victory by landslide and the devil didn't stand a chance, that won't stop him from getting even bolder in your life. Hear me when I say this, the enemy is not done with you. Matthew 12:43-45 ensures us that the enemy grabs some buddies and tries to overtake us by force, but because we are servants of a God who is way more powerful than some dude who was salty because he got kicked out of Heaven. We don't even have to sweat it. God is truly on our side.

The question at this point is will you still be on his? Will you still pray avidly and continue to seek him? Or will you just fall off and come back when things start to become challenging again? Listen here you Fiery soldier of God, do not I repeat DO NOT slip back into lukewarm-ism. (I definitely made that word up) Continue to be on fire for the Lord, continue to seek his face, and continue to do what is right not because of what God can do for you, but simply because of who he is. Because it is surely in our lukewarmism, where the devil has free reign to antagonize our lives and lead us towards the path of destruction.

I am confident in the fact that you, my friend, are going to remain in the army of God and because of your faithfulness to him, he is going to elevate you to greater. A good friend of mine, Natasha Staples, brought my attention to the power of Job 8:7 with her single "Greater Days." It says, "Though your beginnings may seem small, your latter days will be great." Remember dear friend and fellow soldier, this victory is the first of many. The enemy is very calculated, and he will not stop until our final breath, but because we serve an amazing, omnipresent, all knowing, just, and faithful God we are conquerors in any and every situation.

Remove all distraction and sit at the feet of Jesus. Dwell in his presence. Don't immediately begin to speak, but just think of all that he has truly done for you along this journey. Thank him for that because he didn't have to do it, but he did. Allow him to fill your heart, so that there is no room for the enemy to slip in. Ask him to guide your steps and make your paths straight. WHEW!!!! As I write this, I am praying for you, my friend. I am thanking God for the journey and the reward. Enough from me, put this book down and talk to him!!!!

FROM MY HEART, TO YOURS

A Word From The Author

Dear Fellow Solider,

I am so proud of you, words cannot express. You have matured to be a Soldier of Christ who is equipped for any battles that lie ahead. I want to encourage you to continue to seek God in all you do. Continue to love on him as he loves on you. Seek his face each and every day. He is so awesome and has truly shown himself to be mighty through this battle.

Believe it or not, I prayed for you way before this book was ever published. I asked God to send those whom needed to read this book to it. These words are from him and not me, please don't be confused.

I was merely the vessel he chose, which still blows my mind because I am so unworthy.

I challenge you to take what you have learned from this book and share it with others. 1 Chronicles 16 explains that God wants us to shout from the roof tops how awesome he is, spreading his love wherever we go. God doesn't need affirmation, but it shows gratitude and our reverence for him.

The number 1 way we spread Christ is through our day to day lives and actions. It's easy to say that God is good, but when you live life like he is an awesome God, his life shines through you attracting others to him. In all we do we should strive to show Christ.

Remember in all you do, *"Submit to God. Resist the devil, and he will flee."* Live today as if it's your last chance to get it together and be intentional about seeking him. Strive to have a relationship with Christ just as that depicted in Psalm 63.

Love you,

Jerrica

THANK YOU'S

Dad, thank you for being a part of my life. I appreciate how our relationship has grown. I love you dearly, and I can't imagine my life without you.

Tasha, thank you for consistently being a good friend. You came in and pushed me to do things that I never thought I was capable of doing. You encouraged and inspired me to mature and nurture my relationship with Christ each and every day. For that, I am truly grateful. I thank God daily for you. I love you, gal!!

Julian "Cousin," thank you for being intentional about forcing me, (yes forcing) to step outside of my comfort zone. You have truly been there for me and have supported me each step of the way. You have truly motivated me to chase after my dreams. I am so thankful for you. Love you, cousin.

ELW3 "Bishop," thank you for believing in me and giving me that extra push towards the Will of God. Your encouragement has not gone in vain. I have seen such growth in you, and I am proud to call you my brother in Christ. Stay faithful and continue to pursue Christ through it all.

Thank you to my Pastors, Pastor Jamal Oliver and Pastor SinClair Thorne, and a woman who is such an inspiration to me, Minister Felicia Walton. I love y'all and I truly thank ya'll.

Lastly, but certainly not least. To the greatest of them all, My Lord and Savior Jesus Christ. I want to thank God for using me to not only help others achieve freedom but for also helping me to do the same. All the glory, praise, and honor to God!

Stay Connected

Thank you for purchasing, Life without Parole: The Journey to Freedom. Jerrica wants to stay connected with you! Follow her on Facebook, Instagram, and Periscope. For more information on booking, new releases, and speaking engagements, visit: www.trmove.com

FACEBOOK Jerrica Russaw or The Righteous Movement

INSTAGRAM therighteousmovement

PERISCOPE jerricarussaw

www.ingramcontent.com/pod-product-compliance
Lightning Source LLC
Chambersburg PA
CBHW050917160426
43194CB00011B/2442